ARAB HEALTH

With Compliments and Thanks

From

IIR Exhibitions

DUBAI

A PICTORIAL TOUR

WITH PHOTOGRAPHS BY

Charles Crowell, Dubai Civil Aviation, Dubai Duty Free,
Department of Tourism and Commerce Marketing,
Jorge Ferrari, Warren Jackson, Jumeirah International,
Kamran Jebreili, Shirley Kay, Irfan Khan, Klaus Photography,
Alex Livesey, Bob Milne Home, Motivate Publishing,
John Nowell, Otty Studio Library, Adiseshan Shankar,
Mike Shepley and Dariush Zandi.

Published with the
support and
encouragement of

مركز دبي التجاري العالمي
DUBAI WORLD TRADE CENTRE

MOTIVATE
PUBLISHING

Published by Motivate Publishing

Dubai: PO Box 2331, Dubai, UAE
Tel: (+971) 4 282 4060, fax: (+971) 4 282 4436
E-mail: books@motivate.co.ae
www.booksarabia.com

Abu Dhabi: PO Box 43072, Abu Dhabi, UAE
Tel: (+971) 2 627 1666

London: Stewart's Court, 220 Stewart's Road, London, SW8 4UD
E-mail: london@motivate.co.ae

Directors: Obaid Humaid Al Tayer
             Ian Fairservice

Editors: Jackie Nel
             David Steele

Designer: Johnson Machado

© Motivate Publishing 1996, 1999 and 2002

First published 1996
Reprinted 1997
New edition 1999
Reprinted 2000
Third edition 2002

ISBN: 1 873544 99 5

British Library Cataloguing-in-Publication Data. A catalogue record
for this book is available from the British Library.

Printed by Emirates Printing Press, Dubai

INTRODUCTION

from His Highness Sheikh Hamdan bin Rashid Al Maktoum
Deputy Ruler of Dubai, UAE Minister of Finance and Industry
and Chairman of Dubai Municipality.

If you are new to Dubai, welcome – and I hope this book will serve as a useful introduction. And for residents, or visitors who are already familiar with the emirate, I believe it will present some perspectives of our country and history that you may not have seen before.

For those who have recently arrived I suggest that, to get a feel for the place and to begin to understand how and why it works, you take a stroll along the Creek. Appropriately the waterway features large in this book, simply because it has featured large in our history. The activities that occur on and around the Creek exemplify, in microcosm, those of the whole of this industrious, multicultural, adaptable, tolerant city.

The Creek curves through Dubai, its waters reflecting ancient wind-towers and neon advertisements, its skyline alternately punctuated by slender minarets and high-rise offices. Moored at its wharfs or churning its surface are trading dhows and fishing boats, pleasure craft and oil-service vessels. Elegant hotels and handsome gardens line its banks, while the walls of the merchants' houses in the old quarter are still lapped by its tides. Busy along its shores are the people of many nations who live and work here – bringing a cultural variety that enriches every aspect of life in the city.

Geography, of course, has helped. Dubai, positioned midway between Europe and the Far Fast, is at the hub not only of the wealthy Middle East but of a much greater market that stretches from the Levant to the Indian subcontinent and from the newly-emerging states of the CIS to Africa.

But then, throughout the world, strategic locations, especially seaports, have historically been centres of trading activity – although not all have taken full advantage of their position by developing trading skills and supporting services, nor have they all attracted commerce and industry. Those that have – and the most notable examples are Hong Kong and Singapore – have the added ingredient of a liberal regulatory system.

Here in Dubai – while we have, of course, necessary controls and legislation sufficient to secure a fair and just commercial environment – the authorities prefer to leave companies to get on with what they do best: running their businesses.

The success of this policy can be evidenced by a few statistics. In 1958 Dubai's imports totalled some $6 million; in 1968 $168 million; in 2000 $19,346 million. Dubai has always been ready to trade, and to invest in an infrastructure that has already attracted so much commerce and industry to the emirate – ports and cargo facilities, accommodation and telecommunications, modern road systems and an award-winning airline.

In addition to the benefits offered by the city itself, the free zones at Jebel Ali (which has been chosen by more than 2,158 companies from 98 countries as their Gulf base), Dubai International Airport, Dubai Internet City and Dubai Media City have been specifically designed to provide a congenial environment for business. And the needs of the people who live and work here have been equally carefully considered and catered for by the provision of ancillary services, ranging from education to entertainment, sports and leisure facilities to hospitals and clinics, high-quality housing to ease of access for travellers and goods.

While Dubai's history can be traced back some 6,000 years, there has probably been more change in the last three decades than in the whole of the preceding six millennia.

Even as recently as the early 1950s Dubai was still a small entrepôt trading port, the occupants of which, since the decline of the pearl trade a generation earlier, had returned to earning a modest living from the import and re-export of goods. Then, the regular P&O steamships from Bombay would anchor a mile offshore, their cargoes and passengers being unloaded and brought to land by small boats of sufficiently shallow draught to enable them to enter the Creek. And at the desert airstrip the occasional DC3, Heron and Dove would whisk up the sand on the unpaved runways. Few people then could anticipate what immense changes would take place in the years ahead.

But one man could: His Highness Sheikh Rashid bin Saeed Al Maktoum, whose son Sheikh Maktoum so ably continues our late father's policies, combined the shrewdness and trading skills of a merchant with the foresight and imagination of a visionary. If you would like to see his monument then stand at any vantage point in Dubai and look around – not just at the buildings themselves, although they are impressive enough, but also at the people, the activity and the way of life: together they form a unique and still developing testament.

Hamdan bin Rashid Al Maktoum

The United Arab Emirates occupies the southern shores of the Gulf, where the vast expanse of the Rub al Khali – the Empty Quarter – extends for more than 1,000 kilometres across the Arabian Peninsula. Much of the country's 78,000 square kilometres is desert, the dunes reaching heights of 100 metres or more in some parts.

Like the sea, the dunes are in constant motion, being perpetually blown across the landscape at an average rate of about 60 centimetres per year. In the quiet of a desert night you can often hear the whispering of the shifting dunes – and, occasionally, if you're very fortunate, the strange phenomenon of the singing sands when the moving grains strike up choral resonances.

The inhabitants of the region were the Bedu, who coaxed a frugal existence from the reluctant land. With rain falling just 10 days a year, natural vegetation was sparse and theirs was a nomadic existence searching for elusive grazing for their camels and goats. From such a hardy lifestyle in such a harsh environment grew the Arab tradition of hospitality – for a friend in the desert was a friend indeed, with whom water, food and stories would be readily shared.

Dates, rich in nutrients, were a mainstay of the Bedu diet – and the palms from which they came provided a valuable source of materials: the trunk yielded wood for building, the leaf stems were used for fencing and temporary shelter, and the leaves were used for weaving into baskets.

The camel, too, was a cornucopian source of supplies, capable of surviving without water for long periods (losing up to 25 per cent of its body weight without any ill effects). In addition to its role as a beast of burden it also provided meat and milk, wool, skin for water containers and dung for fuel.

Modern development, and the benefits that it's brought, began in earnest in 1966 with the discovery of oil in Dubai's offshore Fateh field. The wealth generated from oil revenues has provided the means for the building of an infrastructure that, in turn, has allowed the more rapid development of the city's traditional role as a centre of commerce and communications and as an entrepôt trading port.

Although written records of Dubai date back only to the late 18th century, there would certainly have been a settlement here long before then because of the Creek – a haven since the earliest days of Arab navigation. Near to the Creek there are now modern container ports, but much local and regional trade is still transported by dhows from the Creek, bringing a sense of history and continuity to the rapidly developing city.

The Creek has shaped Dubai's destiny, and Dubai has shaped the Creek – quite literally. When, in the early 1960s, silt threatened to block the mouth of the waterway and ruin the city's means of trade, the then Ruler, Sheikh Rashid, borrowed US$960,000 – a considerable sum in those pre-oil days – to dredge the channel and construct breakwaters. Now lined by offices, parks and a golf course, tunnelled under, bridged over, and criss-crossed by water taxis, the Creek extends some 15 kilometres inland to where, on the outskirts of the city, the shallow waters are home to flocks of flamingos.

As Dubai evolves, so the contrasts in the landscape become more evident. The slender spires of mosques still pierce the skyline, but they've been joined by high-rise luxury office blocks and hotels. The Creek continues to support working dhows but these are now accompanied by pleasure boats offering dinner cruises with spectacular views of the city.

Dhows moored three and four abreast form a floating city of their own. Still plying routes to India, Pakistan, East Africa and within the Gulf, their cargoes reflect the changing patterns in demand: the romance of spices and perfumes, and trade winds in the lateen rigging, has long since been replaced by the modernity of marine engines and cargoes of electronic goods, furniture, building materials – and even the occasional car or pick-up truck.

At shipyards round the Gulf, dhows are still built in the traditional way. The design and construction follows patterns so well established over the centuries that blueprints are unnecessary. The timber comes mainly from India and, in the hands of skilled shipwrights, it's transformed into sturdy vessels capable of long voyages. While some vessels are equipped with modern navigational aids, most are still steered by the astral methods discovered by Arab sailors 1,000 years ago, which enabled them to venture as far as China in their quest for trade.

The crews are tight-knit bands to whom the dhow is home for months at a time – and they decorate their vessels accordingly. A stroll along the creekside, especially in early evening, reveals much domestic activity, with *hookahs* being smoked, meals being prepared and games being played.

Dubai is really made up of two cities – Bur Dubai and Deira – separated by the Creek. Although now linked by two bridges and a tunnel, by far the most pleasant way of going from one side to the other is by *abra*, the little water-taxis that putter back and forth between the two banks. At Dh 0.50 a trip it must be the best-value sightseeing tour in the world. There's something agreeably old fashioned and leisurely about the *abra* which, amid the traffic and activity of a busy, modern commercial centre, bobs gently about on its mooring while its boatman waits for a full load before setting out on his five-minute voyage. *Abras* can also be hired by the hour for a journey of discovery down to the open sea or following the Creek inland.

The futuristic shapes of the National Bank of Dubai and the Chamber of Commerce and Industry overlook a scene that's changed little for generations. While a traveller from the past would be overawed by the buildings, the sight of the dhows and *abras* would be comfortably familiar.

Dubai's original settlement was founded on the south bank of the Creek and it's in this same area of the city that the Ruler's Diwan is located. From this elegant, traditionally-styled building, adorned with wind-towers and soaring arches, the affairs of the emirate are conducted. It contrasts with the modern architectural forms of the north bank, such as the new elliptical Twin Towers.

Nearby is Bastakiya, the original merchants' district, where many of their distinctive wind-towered houses may still be seen. And at Shindagha, across what used to be a flood-plain at high tide until the land was reclaimed in the 1960s, stands the carefully restored family home of Sheikh Saeed, grandfather of the current Ruler.

Etisalat Tower, topped with an enormous sphere that looks like the hugely magnified result of a misplaced shot from the nearby golf course, is one of Dubai's most distinctive landmarks. Housing high-technology telecommunications equipment, the building is constructed in contemporary materials to an appropriately futuristic design.

In contrast, other buildings combine the latest construction techniques and materials with themes drawn from Islamic architectural heritage – as at the offices of Dubai's Department of Economic Development, where all the advantages of modern accommodation are contained within a framework that recalls traditional local style. The decorative windows and columns and the rich, earthy colours are in sharp contrast with the sleek lines of Etisalat Tower, but each sets off the other – and such juxtapositions provide an exciting cityscape full of surprises.

The Dubai Chamber of Commerce and Industry building dominates the Creek. Its stark, practical, chisel-shaped outline clad in glass captures every change in the light so that, chameleon-like, the building seems to be in a process of continual transformation, just like the city whose interests it represents. With a pleasing sense of continuity in commerce, the building has dhow wharfs at its foot.

Following spread: Before the opening of Al Maktoum Bridge in 1963, vehicles had to make a lengthy detour inland to cross from one side of the city to the other; the original bridge has since been greatly widened. Convenient access between Deira and Bur Dubai is also provided by Al Garhoud Bridge and Shindagha Tunnel.

The Clock Tower, with its fountains and fan palms, is something of a landmark for the city. It stands at one of the busiest intersections in Dubai, where the road leading from Bur Dubai joins the main route from Deira to the airport.

Dubai has established itself as the sporting capital of the entire Gulf region and hosts many world-class events that attract the biggest names in their games. The Dubai Creek Golf and Yacht Club, a 75-hectare oasis of greenery just minutes from the city centre, is one of the hosts of the prestigious annual Desert Classic. It contains two spectacular clubhouses, a marina with its own shipyard, the region's first golf academy, swimming pools, restaurants and bars. The club is a popular venue for entertaining – and with its 18-hole, 6,941-yard, par-72 course, complete with tricky water hazards and deceptive dog-legs, it provides some of the most enjoyable golfing in the world.

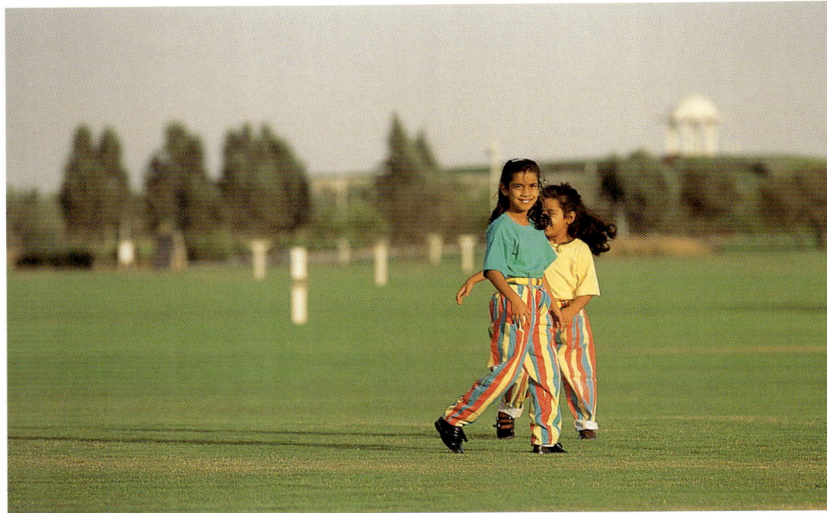

Dubai is a multicultural society and the differing interests and activities of the residents bring colour and variety to every aspect of life. One thing that's common to all, though, is a liking for the city's parks and gardens. This one, just across the Creek from the golf club, is always popular – and especially so when a visiting fun fair sets up, attracting both children and adults to its bright lights and thrilling rides.

The north bank of the Creek has become a showcase for modern architecture but the south side, while also extensively developed, still retains a great many historic buildings in the former merchants' area of Bastakiya.

Early in the 20th century, Iranian merchants transferred their operations to Dubai and settled in Bastakiya, attracted by the city's liberal commercial climate. The merchants brought with them from Iran the concept of the *badgeer*, or wind-tower, an early and effective form of air-conditioning. The square towers are divided diagonally to form four triangular shafts. Any passing breeze builds up air pressure on the windward side while a partial vacuum is created on the leeward, causing air to be pushed down the tower and sucked up again, generating a draught in the room below. Often water would be thrown on the floor beneath the tower, the evaporation of which further cooled the house.

The houses of Bastakiya offer a haven of peace just a few minutes' walk from the busy souks. Plans are well under way to preserve Bastakiya's architectural heritage and restore the houses in the area to their original magnificence. Several of these houses have already been carefully renovated.

Decorative plasterwork above doors and windows was a feature of the houses of wealthier families and good examples may be seen in Bastakiya and at Sheikh Saeed's house in Shindagha.

This house was the home of the ruling Maktoum family until 1958, and is another example of careful restoration. Built of coral blocks and decorated with intricate cornices, carved woodwork and plaster screens, it stands beside the Creek and affords excellent views of the arriving and departing ships.

Wind-towers and large windows allowed the sea breezes to cool the light, high-ceilinged rooms. In addition to family quarters the house has gracious reception rooms – majlis – where citizens could freely come to discuss commercial and other matters with the Sheikh, a tradition of accessibility still continued by members of Dubai's ruling family today.

The massive crenellated walls of Al Fahidi Fort have stood at the centre of Dubai for some 150 years. Apart from its original defensive role, it's been the seat of government, an arms store and the central jail. First opened as a museum in 1971, it's been expanded several times. The most memorable exhibit is the underground gallery containing multi-media presentations and amazingly lifelike dioramas that provide a fascinating insight into the history of Dubai.

Nowhere is Dubai's devotion to trade more obvious than in the old souks. Housed in a maze of narrow streets, often with each trade or commodity concentrated in a specific area, hundreds of small shops compete fiercely for the buyers' custom. Displays of textiles in a tumult of colours, electronic goods, clothing, jewellery, household items, shoes, spices, foodstuffs and dozens of other items all vie for attention. Bargaining is an integral element in most transactions, forming an enjoyable part of the art of shopping.

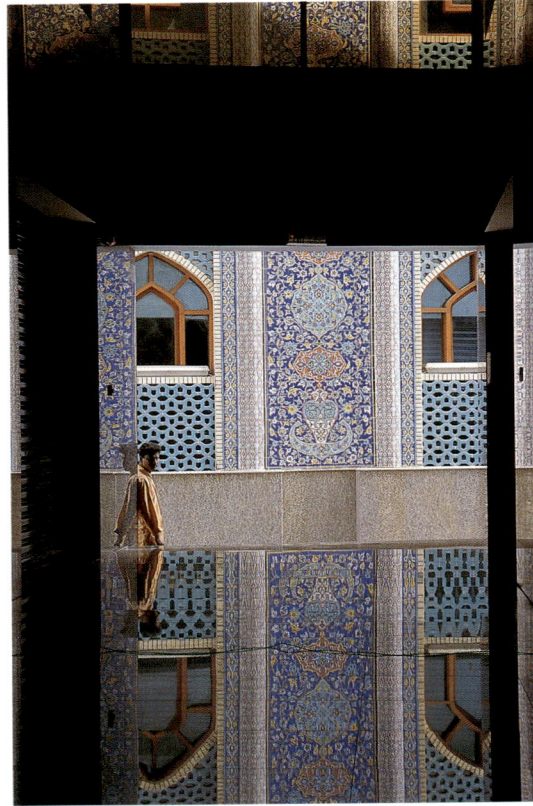

There are plenty of modern, air-conditioned shopping centres in the city, and more are planned. While lacking the atmosphere of the street souks, they're undoubtedly more convenient and comfortable – particularly during the hot summer months. In keeping with the city's liking for fine architecture these new buildings are often of handsome design, such as this one where the highly polished granite floor reflects the intricate patterns of a nearby mosque.

Dubai's best-known market is the Gold Souk. Here visitors walk through a canyon of gold glitteringly displayed in the windows of the small shops that line the covered street. Many of Dubai's early fortunes were based on the gold trade, which boomed when the Indian government, concerned at the drain on its foreign exchange, banned its import in 1947. The trade, considered as smuggling on the subcontinent but entirely legal so far as Dubai was concerned, flourished until the early 1970s when the increase in the oil price and the ensuing worldwide inflation created such a global demand for the metal that ordinary Indian buyers could no longer afford it.

The price of gold is fixed daily and items are sold by weight, there being little or no charge for the often exquisite workmanship. As befits the city's high-tech image, an electronic sign at the entrance to the souk displays the current market rate – and daily confirms Dubai as one of the best places in the world to buy this precious metal.

Following spread: Dubai is a city divided by a waterway, a salt-water inlet known as the Creek – the reason for a settlement being established here in the early days of Arab seafaring. Today, the Creek remains at the heart of Dubai's development as well as its economic life, while still giving the city a unique atmosphere and cachet.

Dubai owes much of its prosperity – and indeed its character – to the sea and the trade routes it provided for the city's merchants. But the abundant natural resources of the warm waters of the Gulf also offered other opportunities.

Pearls were a mainstay of the economy and Dubai's fleet, which once comprised some 300 boats, would set sail for the pearling banks 30 kilometres southwest of the city. At its peak, the trade provided employment for as many as 12,000 people. However, the introduction of the cultured pearl by the Japanese in the 1930s made the trade uneconomical, and the economy was forced to adapt and diversify.

Fishing, too, was an important activity – and remains so today. Snapper, hammour, bonito, mackerel, anchovy and sardines are all plentiful, as are lobsters, crayfish and jumbo prawns. Sport anglers will find plenty to challenge their skill, with sailfish, shark and marlin all providing excellent sport.

Dotted along the coastline are many small fishing villages and ports to which catches are brought aboard a variety of vessels, from the deep-sea *sambuk* to the smaller wooden *houres*. A number of different methods are used by fishermen in the Emirates, including traps, the distinctive igloo shape of which may be seen piled on shorelines and atop dhows headed for the fishing grounds, and seine nets, often hauled ashore by lines of chanting men. The catch is frequently left out in the sun to dry before being packed and sold as fodder or fertiliser.

Fish destined for human consumption are delivered twice daily to the Fish Market at the head of the Creek on Deira-side. Here residents, accustomed to obtaining the freshest of fish, will find many examples still flapping, and the skilled hands of the fishmongers will clean and gut customers' purchases in seconds.

As Dubai has grown, so the urban landscape has expanded. Flyovers, tunnels and expressways have been built; high-rise apartment blocks and luxury hotels sprout from the sand; and towering, glass-façaded office complexes – home to thousands of local and international businesses – reflect the sunlight. These on Sheikh Zayed Road, which leads from the Dubai World Trade Centre to the Abu Dhabi Highway, are among recent additions to an already commanding cityscape. Emirates Towers (left), the tallest building in the Middle East, makes an impressive addition to the Sheikh Zayed Road skyline.

Dubai World Trade Centre (right) is one of the tallest buildings in the Middle East, and is also one of the region's most prestigious addresses. Its 39 storeys house the regional headquarters of many major multinational organisations. The view from the top of the tower, especially at dusk as the city's lights come on, is phenomenal.

The Dubai International Exhibition Centre within the Trade Centre has extensive exhibition facilities. There are now eight halls, which host a wide range of consumer and trade shows. Exhibitors from all over the world come to meet buyers from the Arab Gulf Co-operation Council countries and, increasingly, from even further afield. The Dubai International Congress Centre, a 1,650-seat multi-purpose facility, provides a venue for conferences and live entertainment.

The Trade Centre is easily accessible from within Dubai or from Abu Dhabi, thanks to its position at the end of the burgeoning Sheikh Zayed Road which leads to the Abu Dhabi Highway.

In contrast to the distinctly regional ambience of the souks, the modern air-conditioned shopping malls offer a more international atmosphere. In these mega-malls you'll find shops displaying the finest products from all round the world, with globally-recognised names in the fields of fashion, accessories, perfumes, electronics, furnishings and other consumer goods – all at duty-free prices. Into this world of plenty are attracted residents and visitors alike, assured of both quality and value.

To celebrate Dubai's growing number of modern shopping malls, the city dresses up and organises an annual Shopping Festival. Inaugurated in 1996, it's rapidly become an internationally-known event, attracting visitors from all round the world, and offering thousands of bargains, prize draws and promotions – and some of the lowest prices anywhere. Extravagant entertainments are staged on a daily basis, culminating in a fabulous creekside firework display every evening of the month-long festival.

Quintessential Arabia. Visitors – and residents, too – find that out of the kaleidoscope of images they encounter there are certain evocative moments that capture the essence of the country. Here, as the sun sets across the sea and the muezzin's call echoes from the minarets of Jumeirah Mosque, is one such moment.

Throughout Dubai the urban landscape is interspersed with parks and gardens – many with imaginatively designed play areas for children. Safa Park (above) with its attractive central park and waterfall, is one of the most popular.

Dubai's cosmopolitan population brings a rich diversity to many aspects of life in the city – and the comprehensive educational facilities reflect the differing cultural needs. While government schools provide some of the best education in Arabia – from infant level through to university – private schools cater for different nationalities and their curricula, ensuring children of expatriates may easily transfer back to the educational system in their home country.

With the exception of the height of summer, Dubai's climate positively encourages outdoor life. Even during the heat, walks can be taken along the creekside under shade. While the many sports facilities cater for the energetic, those who take a more leisurely approach to life can enjoy the city's pavement cafés, parks and gardens. In an arid land the softening effect of trees, shrubs and flowers is important and the municipal authorities, in addition to their own greening programme, encourage the private development of gardens by providing free plants.

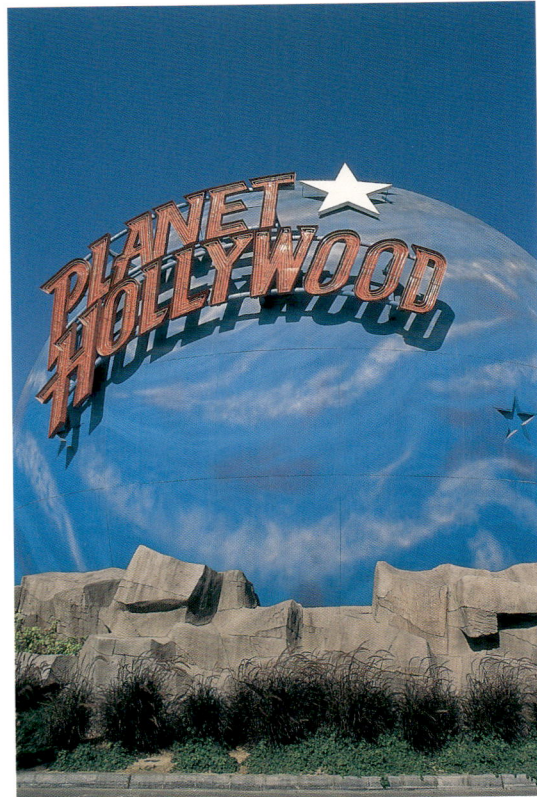

The nightlife can be pretty hot too! As well as the many opportunities Dubai affords to watch traditional Arabic entertainment, the city regularly attracts some of the world's top stars from both East and West – and such acts draw large audiences from an increasing number of neighbouring countries.

Many restaurants also provide live music in the evenings; among these are the world-famous chains, Hard Rock Café and Planet Hollywood. Just like the range of amusements, the cuisine served in Dubai's hotels is completely international and diners could choose a different restaurant for every night of the year.

Recovery from night-time excesses in Dubai is simple. Remaining healthy and fit is made easier by the facilities at the numerous hotels and sports clubs. There are now also several health spas, one of the most prestigious being The Pyramids, a replica of an Egyptian pyramid, surrounded by giant Egyptian statues and crouching sphinxes. Housing the largest professional day spa in the United Arab Emirates and offering all kinds of relaxation therapy, this complex also includes three restaurants, a nightclub and a health club.

Leisure activities for the more active are often water-based, ranging from scuba-diving through water-skiing to more traditional sailing.

The sea – once the domain of fishermen and pearl-divers – now makes a further contribution to the economy through the development of leisure travel. Miles of uncrowded, sandy beaches lapped by the warm, safe waters of the Arabian Gulf are ideal for water sports of all kinds on or below the waves. These features, combined with the emirate's many other attractions, have helped to establish Dubai as a popular destination among discerning travellers. The city is now ever-increasingly featured in the programmes of leading tour operators.

Dubai's superb resort hotels such as the Burj Al Arab provide their guests with direct access to the sea, as well as a wide choice of other facilities, presenting visitors with the difficult task of selecting what to do next: the beach? the pool, agreeably augmented by a swim-in bar? water sports or tennis? Decisions also extend to selecting from the many tempting restaurants. Or an evening in the desert. Or a night club. The choice is yours.

At several hotels boats may be hired for a day's angling or merely lazing on deck. Even city-centre hotels take advantage of the proximity of the sea.

Even the architecture of some of Dubai's hotels reflects its seafaring heritage. The Jumeirah Beach Hotel has been imaginatively designed to resemble a giant wave and has quickly become one of the city's outstanding architectural landmarks. Three hundred metres long and 'cresting' at a height of 100 metres, the wave rises dramatically out of lavishly landscaped gardens. Its companion, the exclusive Burj Al Arab, is a 202-suite tower hotel located on a man-made offshore island. Continuing the nautical theme, the 'Burj' is built to duplicate a dhow in full sail. A resort complex, the hotel even has its own marina and health club, which includes the exclusive Assawan Spa.

Arabs have sailed these sunlit seas for thousands of years and a scene such as this possesses a timeless quality. Even in a place changing as rapidly as Dubai, it seems, there are still constants.

The sea is not always so peaceful. As well as many regional powerboat meetings, Dubai hosts two major races in the UIM Class One World Powerboat Championship series, attracting entrants – and spectators – from all over the world. The UAE's own Victory Team has collected many international trophies.

Jet-skiing and speedboating, too, are sports with a rapidly increasing following. The machines can be rented at a number of locations – offering white-knuckle rides over the waves.

And for the younger generation, the Wild Wadi complex near The Jumeirah Beach Hotel is a popular water-theme park with thrilling rides, exciting slides and pools.

Dubai's reputation as the sporting capital of the Middle East is well deserved. Emirates Golf Club had the first of Dubai's four grassed courses (and indeed the first in the whole of the Middle East) which was completed in 1988 – until then it was merely a stretch of desert. Now its 70 hectares of honed greens, fish-filled lakes and palm-edged fairways play host to many of golf's greatest names, attracted by the superb winter climate and the excellence of both 18-hole courses. It is also one of the hosts of the prestigious annual Desert Classic tournament.

In addition to championship golf, Dubai is the venue for many other world-class sporting occasions, such as the ATP Dubai Tennis Open (left), the Dubai Sevens – one of the largest Rugby Sevens meetings in the world (above), the Dubai International Rally and dozens of other events including snooker, sailing, cricket, football and horse-racing.

Dubai's association with horse-racing is strong. The ruling Al Maktoum family has acquired a formidable reputation, their horses regularly winning some of the most prestigious races in the world calendar. Nad Al Sheba Racecourse, just minutes from the city centre, offers superb facilities for horses, riders and spectators and is the venue for one of the world's richest horse-races – the Dubai World Cup, held in March. Run over 10 furlongs (2,000 metres), the race is for four-year-olds and upwards.

In its short history, the Dubai World Cup has been a spectacular success, attracting crowds of up to 30,000 people to Nad Al Sheba Racecourse. Not only has the race drawn many international competitors, but it's also been won by some of the world's greatest champion horses, including the legendary Cigar, Singspiel, Silver Charm and Dubai Millennium.

Camel racing, too, attracts huge – and hugely enthusiastic – crowds, whether to the racecourses on the outskirts of the city or to the more informal country circuits.

While camels were once an essential ally in the struggle to survive in the desert, many are now bred exclusively for racing – and good beasts can command high prices. Tough animals they are too, with races of up to 16 kilometres providing a test of stamina as well as speed. Camels are less easy to control than horses, and the scene at the start can appear chaotic with camels, riders, trainers and owners occasionally disappearing in the miniature sandstorm created by restless hooves. The races are followed with great interest by all spectators, young and old alike.

Desert safaris, including dune-driving, sand-skiing, desert feasts – and the chance to ride a camel – are popular on any tourist itinerary; very occasionally racing camels may be seen in the desert, being exercised by their trainers and conjuring up romantic images of the nomadic Bedu of old.

Despite the harsh conditions in the desert and mountains, there are many indigenous species of animals – although, as in other parts of the world, modern development is encroaching on their habitats. The UAE authorities have set up conservation programmes to minimise the damaging effects of modern society and, in some cases, captive-breeding programmes have been introduced. A particular success has been the Arabian oryx, which has been saved from extinction by local efforts – and has been adopted as the symbol of the International Fauna and Flora Preservation Society.

Falconry is a popular traditional sport in the Emirates. While the actual hunt takes place in the desert the final stage of the falcon's training includes being brought into town so that the bird becomes used to noise and crowds – although this is a very rare sight today. So highly regarded is the falcon that Dubai has a veterinary hospital dedicated exclusively to the bird's welfare.

While the advantages of a modern, urban society have been welcomed, the ancient traditions of Arabia are still practised in everyday life, particularly during family and religious celebrations. A wedding is the occasion for some of the most colourful festivities, when the bride's house is decorated with thousands of coloured lights draped over the building. The reception can last for three days or more.

Men and women usually gather separately and classical dances feature prominently in the celebrations. Men stand in two opposite rows, clashing their camel sticks, or sometimes swords, while chanting and swaying in time to the rhythm of drums. Women often perform an elegant dance, swirling their long hair with graceful movements of their heads.

Traditional musical instruments reflect the materials of earlier times – drums made from animal skins, goats' hooves attached to a belt which clack and rattle with every movement, and bagpipes made from a goat's stomach.

Dubai is understandably proud of its cultural heritage and works hard at preserving its customs.

A traditional heritage village with wind-tower houses is located near the mouth of Dubai Creek in the Shindagha district. In addition to exhibits on pearl-diving and irrigation techniques, it features artists practising time-honoured crafts as well as dancing displays.

Power to the people. The increasing demands of industrial, commercial and domestic electricity consumers are met by an efficient generation and distribution system.

In Dubai itself there is little obvious evidence of the oil and gas industry. Rig-support vessels may be seen in the Creek, but there are no refineries or shore terminals to be seen. All but one of Dubai's oilfields lie offshore, the sole onshore field being shared with Sharjah.

Dubai uses an innovative method of transporting oil to shore, which avoids building costly under-sea pipelines. Crude oil is stored at sea in *khazzans* – huge, submerged tanks that look like inverted glasses – from where it's loaded directly into tankers.

The Dubai Government is well aware of the fact that the emirate's reserves are non-renewable and will run out one day. Much emphasis has been placed on the use of revenues to establish and develop an economic infrastructure which will reduce dependence on oil and gas and minimise the impact that their price fluctuations have on the economy. Testimony to the success of this carefully planned diversification programme is the fact that the value of Dubai's non-oil exports now exceeds those of the petroleum sector.

The city is the region's prime transportation centre; long established as a major seaport (now with a dedicated cruise-liner terminal), it's also served by the Middle East's busiest airport. The award-winning Dubai International Airport is as vital to the city's commercial activities as the Creek. Some 100 carriers link Dubai to more than 130 cities around the globe. In addition to looking after 15-million passengers a year, the airport also handles 582,000 tonnes of air-freight through its cargo terminal. The Dubai Airport Free Zone, covering an area of more than one-million square metres, was designed to promote high-tech manufacturing and consolidate Dubai's position as the region's pivotal business hub.

The airport is also the home base of Emirates, the international airline of the UAE. Emirates commenced operations in 1985 with three regional routes and by 2002 served 60 destinations. The airline has established a reputation for high standards and innovative service and has also won myriad international awards. Another award winner based at Dubai International Airport is Dubai Duty Free, which occupies the largest single retail space in Dubai and sits firmly within the top-10 listing of the world's airport shops.

While the Creek and the harbour at Hamriya provide wharfage for dhows, modern container vessels, bulk carriers and other vessels require more sophisticated facilities. Port Rashid is located within the city and includes a new cruise-ship terminal. Jebel Ali Port – the world's largest man-made harbour, so huge that it's visible from space – has 67 berths, and lies 30 kilometres to the southwest. Both offer sophisticated handling and storage facilities and work closely with Dubai Airport to further develop the rapidly increasing volume of sea-air business.

At Jebel Ali is the free zone, a commercial and industrial area which provides companies with a range of benefits that include 100 per cent foreign ownership, no corporate taxes and sponsorship of employees undertaken by the Free Zone Authority. So attractive is this environment that the number of investors in the free zone soared from less than 300 in 1990 to 2,158 from 98 different countries in 2001.

Dubai's maritime expertise has been expanded to include ship maintenance and repair. The Dubai Dry Docks, completed in the late 1970s, is among the world's largest and can accommodate vessels of up to one-million tonnes. Other yards on the Creek have facilities for smaller vessels and are busy with oil-support tugs, dredgers and dhows.

The diversification of Dubai's economic base has proceeded rapidly. Light manufacturing, plastic fabrication, food processing and packaging, cable manufacturing and garment-making have all been successfully established.

The biggest non-oil industrial company is Dubal, which produces high-grade aluminium from an energy-efficient complex that, in addition to a smelter, includes a power station and desalination plant – the energy from the smelting operation being recycled in the desalination process.

Whatever exciting developments may be under way in the city, the desert has a permanence of its own – as well as an unfailing attraction for visitors.

Many parts of the UAE could, until recently, be reached only by camel. Now even remote areas have been made accessible by fine roads that slice across the desert and through mountain passes.

Despite the arrival of cars and trucks the camel can still be found in large numbers, and it has a propensity for wandering out in front of cars in the middle of highways – a habit that does neither party any good.

Sand, when shaped by wind and the occasional rains, can take on extraordinary patterns and shapes, some abstract and flowing, others of a geometrical precision that look as solid and permanent as the rock from which, tens of thousands of years ago, the sand was formed. Dune sand – low in salts and high in silica – is commercially extracted and used as aggregate in the manufacture of high-quality cement.

For visitors, who often expect nothing but flat desert, the varied topography comes as something of a surprise. The mountain ridges are barren but beautiful, with picturesque villages deep in the valleys. And the desert itself comprises many different landscapes, the colour of the dunes varying from pale cream near the sea to deep red inland. The height and form of the dunes change too, depending on the prevailing wind and the size and shape of the individual grains of sand, so that some are mere gentle undulations while others tower 100 metres or more, their knife-edge crests describing a perfect parabola against the sky.

Two perspectives of Dubai's mountainous landscape. Above, the valley is tamed by the sweeping lawns and colourful gardens of the Hatta Fort Hotel, an oasis of luxury where fine food, music and dancing, a swimming pool and a range of sporting activities provide all the pleasures of modern living.

On the right the scene has not changed in centuries and the mountains are remote and wild. In the wadi, gouged out by winter rains, trees maintain a precarious hold, while high above the barren crests bake in the sun.

In few parts of the world has there been such dramatic change in such a short space of time, yet all this has been achieved without fundamental alteration to established values and conventions. Here in the emirate of Dubai the best of the new has been successfully combined with the long-established traditions of the country, enabling the next generation to benefit from recent developments without having to forego the security and sense of continuity that comes from stability in social, family and religious matters.

PHOTOGRAPHIC CREDITS

ACKNOWLEDGEMENTS

The publishers would like to thank all the photographers who contributed their memorable images for this book and Bob Milne Home in particular, who not only provided a number of photographs, but also wrote the book's commentaries. Also, the Dubai World Trade Centre, without whose sponsorship support the publication of this book would not have been possible.

مركز دبي التجاري العالمي
DUBAI WORLD TRADE CENTRE